Two Murals

Jesús Castillo

The Song Cave

The Song Cave
www.the-song-cave.com
© Jesús Castillo, 2021

Design and layout by Janet Evans-Scanlon

ISBN: 978-1-7372775-1-4
Library of Congress Control Number: 2021943882

FIRST EDITION

Contents

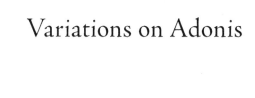

Variations on Adonis

So what do we write then, and how?
Is there meaning for what will not enter language?
And why are the mind's sorrows mere graves for the body's desires?

—We will not succeed at writing anything
unless we see it
staring back at us.

—Writing that has no chasms, has no identity.

—ADONIS

This is forgetfulness: that you remember the past
and not remember tomorrow in the story

—MAHMOUD DARWISH

I will call this city a sad marionette
And call the continent's shorelines roving wolves
(A bird or a sky perhaps
will be born from the naming)
And I'll call the desert sun an oak tree
Maybe the sea will wake and become a child
or the dream of a child in whose mind the future buries itself

There's nothing left to clean the cuts in my voice
The crowds of bystanders will pass
and night will come with its raids

There are monsters in the water
like there are monsters in our dreams

Turning the pages of a wasteful age
        under a netnerved sky,
        these are my steps:

Take warmth from loved ones, steadiness
from clouds, spend all of it on winter.

When the day's ration of hope is drained
    my night begins in earnest.

The city blends with the swivels of my eyes.
    I drink for the flowers
        planted in your words

Whatever fashioned us, its fashioning was nothing
        but a woken leaf
    shaken by the vision of itself dissolving.

Ages of us became paper to burn in the State's houses
        and the urban camps in winter.

I watched abundance destroy itself,
and still we led everyday lives through the waste
        and slaughter.
Just today, for example, I'm riding a southbound train,
drinking beer and watching the coastline glitter by.

The mountains seldom speak
but they spoke thus:

    We hold the future waterlines and dwelling nooks
    of any ambling race that can survive.

    The crust of the human will crumple in its casket,
    give way to certain birds and a salamander's dream.

My veins pulse, hopeful

Dear Empire, I am confused each time I wake inside you.
    You invent addictions.
Are you a high-end graveyard or a child?
    I see your children dragging their brains along.
    Why not a god who loves water and dancing
        instead of mirrors that recite your pretty features only?

You wear a different face to each atrocity.
You are un-unified and tangled.
    Are you just gluttony?
    Are you civilization's slow grenade?

I am confused each time I'm swallowed by your doors

And the women work to wake each other up
    in the midst of history swiveling.

The women hoist the day up from the well,
braid their expenses, singing: 'God is the rotted plants
    that feed the June bugs, the swallowing
    and birthing of the world
    and we are its hands.'

And they asked the sky: 'Is this world fodder
    or a seed?'
And they unsewed the sky.
And from the punctures in the air

Life paused at the doorway of a book that dissolved
    on a sidewalk in Manhattan.
Some had not heard yet: *From Lot's days to Hiroshima*
    the wasteland is the same.

Delusions become mountains of facts.

Here I loved a stunted apple tree left
between highways,
    a wandering train station
    and the young who danced
    on song's ashes.

God plays in the eternity of childhood as God plays
    in the light that washes the days.
The war machines sigh with spent bodies
and the future is a ghost we must inhabit,
    make alive.
Screens paint illusions that loss
snips, and yet some of us insist
on sleep without dreams.

               In a city of synthetic moods
the children fight dreamlessness with music. They uproot
dream's veins and change the air of waking:

Let sky and earth and man trade limbs.

This land lives in the belly of a caged cow
with swollen ankles, marked for the steel bolt.
It yearns for the putridness of the earth.
A cleansing. It spasms on the floor of its factory.

I see a sound, a cry.
Our cities are fantasies around it,
scaffolds for skittish minds.

Celan survived a nightmare to end in its mutations.
Did he have at least a memory of sweetness
        to fall towards at the edge of his river?
A poet releases his voice and becomes a child.
His voice is the dream, the dreamer
and the hunger inciting him.
When it is done with him
he goes back to his bed of grass by the stream.

My hands were branches that abandoned their leaves.
In their veins was a dream of a world I had heard
        in a mother's song :
there were leviathans that swam between the ice floes
        and wanted nothing but to mate
        and spread their songs in the seas.

Like this I entered your city
   and waited for our meeting in the park,
   with jarfuls of song
   for your laughter and your hair
   your childlike face
   and eyes full of daybreak.

I love summer's heat and openness.
The eternity of insects that are gone
follows me from the café patio to the plaza.
The day's light is a robe our gaze wears.

From time to time my happiness surprises me:
    a little raft appearing round a bend in the rapids.
I entered the symposium of the grass.

The city waited for me to grow tired
of my vastness under the open sky.

Waited and waited.

Having reached the geologic timescales,
we have all these new ways of unthreading the tapestry,
        reweaving it into extinctions and war's endless gadgets.

I sit with the warmth of a cup of coffee
        on a winter morning at my mother's house
        and I write to spring:
Give me the names of our victims and their shapes.
Give me a train and a window
        opened to the radiant day
        any day
and I'll not shy from life's accounting

And the day's pages shine for new lovers
and the storms that dance with them the dance
of scattered lives.

In the tent of my pleasures, I walk
  past plastic bottles
  and bees searching
  for their flowers.

How do we apologize to animals we drowned?

Missed calls. A face opening at the sight of another.
Light's pages. The cries language can't explain.

Who am I to say the truth? How do I paint for you the warmth
    of the memory of you smiling at me smiling for no reason
    than us sitting in the murmur and soft movements
    of a café tucked in one of the city's canyons,
    together awhile before parting again into separate lives?

Your memory as I sit alone now in this yard in California
    watching the lake and the hills and the orange sky falling
    behind them?

Shining and wild is our blood's call.
    Like sunflowers in summer, in a field by a small town
    after the war has passed
    and gone to join the other wars in the world's crucibles.

How do we give a starfish its last taste of salt?

How can withered trees blossom?
And when did the flood season arrive? Did we not feel it?
The atmosphere smears the Arctic and the Earth flows
        luxuriant, carrying our shores in its giant hands.
And we did not feel it.

A festival springs from the corpse of a lake
in this four-legged civilization.

I sit on a patch of grass, in the shade of a skyscraper,
counting the pulses in my temple
the pores in my daydream.

How can withered trees blossom?

I make a little grave for their absent shadows, feel the ground
against my palms, and stand (I have other towns to see,
other seasons to inhale up close).

A mango tree wakes me in the village of innocence
where the silence of the dew left by the rain gave way
as we talked about love on our way to the fields.

And the fields became a fleeting impulse in the eyes
    of a child hungry for the body's terrors
    as he passed by on a crowded bus.
His eyes met the deceitfulness of light in the city
    where the workers dream.
    And the child wandered, pure as violence,
    in the music of sped-up days.

But I, unlike him, have no taste for fame:
I'm but a shadow
        watching from pockets in the crowd.
My hands are branches, and my eyes close
to wake me in the village of innocence.

Who is there to shake the First World?
To pierce its excess and boredom?
Its mind is its enemies' best war machine,
a porous mind that anxiety feeds.

A pair of lovers wakes in California,
          years before the firestorm,
the devastation already in their limbs, wrapped
in their trust of each other's time.

As the air rotted we danced in our rooms.
So do not say: Poetry was a rose that became blood.
Say: Earth forces man to face man
          and collects the accounts payable
          from war's entrails to sow the next day
          where lovers are sleeping
          while the sky storms its story.

The voice of our victims is silence we talk around
    at dinner,
though we're all siblings, like the locusts and leaves
and the moisture at work in the pores of the forest.

A dolphin wove a melody under the warship
    on the eve of the assault.
It was a bright blue morning
    and the fishermen chanted a hymn as they hacked off
    the fins of live fish.

And a child wandered an empty beach
    and heard a voice that asked: Are you my voice?
And the child answered: My voice is my time.
    I uproot the veins of my father's dream
    to make a bay for my night in the night of the world.
    My voice and I tell each other stories
    so we can laugh and row to sunrise.

There's nothing between migrant and patriot
    but a generation and its threads
    claiming colors for their days.

Claiming no colors but the ones that drift
    beautifully past me into the memory of words
    I exist,
outside both my nations
as I drive their roads and wander their markets,

my senses my horses, my body a chariot searching
for its immortality before the Earth
claims it for its musk and its trees' seeds.

The Empire's statesmen polish their pens between regimes.
Somewhere Lincoln leads his people past genocide's fields
and Juarez becomes a statue gazing forever
at his country's red horizon.

The desert that straddles two nations was the thread
    I was torn from
and its cities are my pagan chandeliers.

So the story begins, or so the story ends.

Every thing blossoms into human existence
    through the eyes of a word: hydrogen, ceasefires, touchscreens,
    tulips, containment, bureaucracy, satellites,
    plum brandy, centuries, sand.

What words birthed your father's father?
What did he say to your grandmother
    when he first approached her by the well to confess his wish,
    both of them youths, the generations in them merely waves
    of nervousness and tension in their nimble limbs?

What words spilled from her on that first night they braved?
What words when they opened the window
    and let the vision of a new day take them?

Beauty is a migrant whose home has no language.
It breathes negation, affirming the soil and the rain
    and the losses that shape its disguises.

In the Empire's academies life was easy.
We built our cities of words in heated rooms in Winter.
Spring and Summer were twin festivals of flesh
and lush green lawns, and Fall was an opera house
           that cast showers of leaves.

We lost our minds because we could
and found them waiting for us with a patient smile
on a walk through the cemetery.

Our sex was a game we played
against time's tide, and poetry was a sacrificial bird
in our meetings at the bar.

When I left, I painted the cities in my notebook
the way the alphabet paints the mind's impressions
into shells of ink. I painted them
not to heal a wound or re-enliven Whitman's ghost
but to reclaim our differences. To cleave bridges,
to bathe the mutilated culture and sift
through the hemorrhaging inheritance
it left us.

From the roads of a subjugated country
    declawed by its awe of the conqueror's wealth
I set out to undress my history.

Let us speak frankly, Mexico's towns.
We know our statesmen sold our veins
to decorate their silverware. Ours is a self-
mutilated land of hybrid people born
in a savage time.

We must carve our way out of shame's corpse.
We don't need to ask forgiveness on Sundays.
There is no shame out here, in the porous world.
This borderless place built on bodies.

And I sang the cities,
    like a lover carrying his love to his chosen end.
My language was a bag of stones
casting echoes at the buildings.

We invaded the sky with our astounding irrelevance.
We walk in electronic brains that span the whole globe
    and I question their light.

To our dear Empire, I say: the spell of your history has faded.
Forget holidays and safety nets
    and learn like your old frontiersmen to tread carefully
    on the soil of a New World.
One becomes prolific at enslavement and wakes one day
    inside a steel security camera.

One invents the human toy
    and becomes its addict.

Your running water, your sports teams, your cancer treatments, your personalized entertainment streams, libraries, co-ops, academies, pop songs, your free speech, your space stations, satellites, wide freeways and clean coastal towns, your research labs, drones, Christmas Balls, shopping sprees, cell towers, barbeques, your bright organic produce aisles, your cotton shirts and tennis shoes, electric cars, your fitness clubs, your museums: are these

the fruits of your chaos?

Is this why we bleed the world's harvest, why we must live amidst this branded trash? Why do your young men grow confused and homicidal in their rooms?

. . . from a desert that binds two countries . . . etc.
In which decadence enters, a master, riding an animal
the size of a prison before turning into statues and street signs.
In which Justice wipes her ass (or she used to) while around her
men and women wander a body the color of asphalt
and screens play shots of radiant-skinned mannequins running
through sunkissed, dirtless fields while cigarette ash gets lost
in a sidewalk's night.   Here

> *safety*   is a house roofed with corpses
> *love*   is an animal dragged through the market for ages
> *the self*   a chimera lost in its voices
> *the sun*   a knife that brushes skin cells off vagabonds and migrants
>   arriving from a desert that lays bare the chests
>   of two countries . . . etc.

On the dance floor, the heat of your body played a game
  with the heat of my hands.
Our skin young and fleeing its history lessons
  toward its animal wish.
Your fingers on my face, we made a little cave for our breath
  in the crowd, as speakers spilled their electric seas
  and the floor pulsed under us like an artery.

And for a while we were only our bodies
  and my field of vision was your hair against our cheeks
  and exchanged mouths.

Outside, in our winter jackets, faces flushed, holding hands,
we exchanged middle names, shared a cigarette and waited
for a cab that years later became a little boat in a dream I woke from,
alone, on a road that lead to an unknown shore
  under a sky full of questions.

Love landed on the wings of a bird building its nest
    in the ruins of a combat tank.
The image birthed thousands of images shared and forgotten
    and Love continued unhurried through the air above the fields,
waving its music, inciting the animals into the smoke-filled season.

And in the mountains where the air is clear
    Love luxuriated in the cold, cold birthplace of a river.
Trees bearing the fruits of change and migration
    tossed their celebrations at the sun, their branches windows.

And Love lay down to dream under a pine.
And as it slept a pair of sparrows learned to launch their songs
    above the noise of construction crews
and far away a black bear scavenged in canyons of ice.

O Walt Whitman . . . how could the slave have been the same in sleep
    as his master?
What each sleeper's waking body hauls into the land of sleep
    shapes his dreams.

We know the waking body of the master got to dine with his children
    and wife, and smoke tobacco on his porch while he discussed the harvest
    or the next election or rumors of revolts in the Carolinas or New Orleans.
We know the waking body of the slave was mutilated
    and saw the mutilation of bodies like it. That it labored to exhaustion
    beneath hot, indifferent suns, and may have been sold away
    from the bodies of his family oceans ago.

So what do you think the dreams of each were like?
What do you think swam beneath the sleepers' twin expressions
    of restlessness or peace? Were they both falling?
And do you think the slave's nightmares needed sleep's help
    to flood his senses?

I question the light and leave,
  lugging my history from station
  to station like a bag of ripe cactus flowers.

They taught me this land was worth dying for,
worth the bloody mixing of the races
that collided in the lush valley.

They taught me I have brothers in El Salvador and Chile,
  that the borders of our land are far north
  where the trees are tall and red.

They taught me this land was worth the burning
  of a whole civilization.

So why do I see only this red factory on the horizon?

New York—Central Park—Penn Station—5th Avenue

"Laziness resembling work, work resembling laziness."
    Every meeting an exhibit of private dramas to color the hours.
Markets that follow you in sleep. Slaves of every race. The world's art
    amassed in high-roofed vaults where the fashionable stroll
    amongst the marble
    and school children glimpse the astonishing beauty
    bought by missiles and signatures.

Here on the plush side of the planet, the gutters are aflood with plastic and
    electric signs. And the steam that rises from the gratings
    is another citizen of the glutted night.
And there are rats in Mexico City and elsewhere, dressed in White House
    cotton, armed with documents, gnawing at the land.

The jester, horrified when the world became a comedy,
    died on the banquet table.
The jester died but the comedy did not. He died
    like the pleas in the lungs of the drowned.
    Like water vanishing into the desert's cracked floor
    or a butterfly in a cobweb after a failed migration.

He was like the others who came after.
He ended and the comedy did not
    and in his last breath he left a poison
    for the others.

I began from here, by the image of a demolished house
            during my morning coffee, a house
            of shells and washed-out pictures.

I began from here.
            From the clatter of the market on Monday,
            the flood of doctored stories and advertised
                        selves on the sides of buildings,
            from a country that spills graves like a drunk giant.

Begin from here, a voice said, the way rivers begin.
The way water enters emptiness
                                    and seeks a shape.

But I am the same as you, Walt, when I sleep.
I sleep and am happy if it's on a soft bed
or with a good blanket on the floor of a friend's apartment.

And when I am awake, I am like you.
I too marvel that men and women like us existed,
were flexible and real and alive.
To think of those long ago idylls of peace between wars
and even in the midst of wars
when love flooded towns and birthed generations.

To think we were not there to see and feel and bear our part.
To think we are here now, and bear our part.

And I want to live. I have work to do before my harvest.

When I step on the field
    it blooms with questions. Its disasters open
to reveal blood reaching, still, for a tomorrow
that will pour its nectar in the mouths
    of its children.

We want to live, they say.
We read our textbooks
    and iron our school uniforms every night
    before bed.
We dutifully learn the names of the world you gave us.

We live. We have games to lodge
into the maelstrom.

A Mural After Darwish

I want to be naked with you, she said
as her dog ran ahead of us and vanished
into the tall brush.

I could see to our left across the lake
the top of an old weather tower jutting above the treetops.
A hummingbird's flight over the water
carried me to another childhood.
The sunlight as we crossed the marsh
caught the back of her neck as it was inscribing itself
in my memory.
I would become someone else.
A man in a chair by a window
remembering this day as bright:
the white contrail in the clear sky,
the yellow leaves like tiny suns floating
from branches,
a beetle's green armor
darting by.
I walked in a body eager
from wasted days,
wondering if there'd be in the end
some angel to demand:
What did you become?
What did you do there, in life?

And I wondered,
Will a friend guide me at the edge of my life
to the city of the dead?
In non-being: no gates or walls, no songs
or thoughts of them. Though no lack either
in non-time.

Hours later we made our way back
to the parking lot, her dog appearing
from the bushes, tongue bathed in prey.
I ran my hands through her fur, my fingers
obsessed and speechless.

Like this I live inside myself
in the net-nerved air of this place,
my muscles and bones in the prime of death
and the notes in my voice collecting paints.

Someday I'll become what I was.

I'll become an idea.
No screens will show my face.
No rockets will carry me to the wastelands
of mud and glass. I'll be
neither call nor echo
but the endless distance.
Lighting a cigarette with another cigarette,
a night turns into day.

And someday I'll become what I've seen.

I'll become a hummingbird.
I'll unsheathe my wings out of my void
and dart across lakes, taking my reflection with me,
my flight imprinted into onlookers' eyes.
I am the dialogue of dreaming.
Meaning blinded me and disappeared.
I am absence awake on its other shore.

And someday I'll become what I want.

I'll become a poet
and wander the same sidewalks, restrooms, bars, beaches.
I'll carry my dreams under my tongue
and go on writing inside my decay.
The transitions between light and dark
will be my vision's subject.
I won't point to my perceptions. Perceptions
are my pretext (I come from them).
And when they leave

I'll become what I was.

I'll become a sugar cane field.
So let the sun press summer from me
and the factories burn my leaves

and those passing along the dirt road
cut my stalks.

Someday I'll become what I was.

And she said, I see you there
singing in the basement of your brain
before a window opened to your daydream's sky.
Come. We're still here in the blatant light
of the afternoon. The edge
is sharp and unforgiving
so be a firm ghost to your body's child.
Inhabit the body to exhaustion.
Even as it ages its needs are the same.
Bring home to it your findings.

We walked again in the woods.
No one around, only more marshes up ahead
along the water. A few yards inland,
on a patch of moist bark and dark leaves
we lay down.

Sunlight glinted on her lips
as I pulled down the straps of her dress and found
no words to describe her firm softness, or later how the earth
anchored our bodies as they moved.

Someday we'll become what we were:

slipper animalcules
ciliated
in the coat of arms . . .
bodied, late-morning creatures
walking barefoot across hallways,
the other asleep in our bed.
Washing faces before mirrors,
thinking these many years are locked in us and gone.
Drinking tea before the news,
the nations morphing into nations
as our flags go on trial for shortsightedness
and the whole earth is an executioner's sword.

And of the trees I only know the eucalyptus
swaying its branches over a field behind my mother's house.
In the middle-distance a road leading to a freeway
that goes north along the ocean.
So let's sit on this bench and watch
the cars pass, the sun fall, til the clouds ashen
and night turns to us.

My poem's land is woven, crossed
south to north by mountains passing through forests
and deserts, all scattered with infinite interiors:
paved-over grounds traversed by automated lives,
veined by cables and roads that rise to the halogen

faces of buildings totemic and glass.
And from the edges of the cities where the fields begin
my poem solicits the company of breezes and insects
and the solitude of those sitting in the passing planes
looking down at our lights: the speech of people
whose old gods have fled.

In a warm room at night
a woman asks for her femininity,
gets up from her bed to visit her beauty
and binds her hair with a steel dragonfly.
And she toys with her poet.
I want to be a gazelle against your palm, she says,
and let my eyes go blind beside your sleep.
All I have of me tonight is this wish to be adored,
so give me your gaze and your hands' warmth
and leave us alone.
Nothing goes with you
and nothing comes back.

And the poet says, Take my art if you want.
There's nothing in it for me besides you.
The objects in my poems age and vanish like real objects
and cadence doesn't come from the words
but the opposing solitudes of bodies in a night.
We trade echoes and in the morning, uncertain, we ask:
Which one of us is "I"?
I'll be its other. A rain will play

between words and actions and my hands
will remember their days.

I came from a village of stone wells
and news of space stations we saw
mostly through black and white screens.
There was quick violent death to be had
in drunk towns and arid mountains, and death
to be had under open skies, among trees.
As now, there was also the prolonged death of hospitals
and the remote death of impersonal wars,
those buttons that work perfectly.

So what sleeplessness brought you here love?
Tell me your wound and together we'll gain
and lose our roads twice.
You lure me back to life and fracture my outlines.
So I stay and let my blood cells' aging
spend me, and the radiated air dissolve me
'til I enter the waves and their cold December crashes
wake me back into my skin.

I am driving down the California coast.
The houses lounge in the breeze
while inside them stream live shots of other lives
exploding in the sun across the sea.

Here on these clean streets
a late-imperial Narcissus wanders under balconies
saying, I love me in this picture.
I'll be a virtuoso when it comes to my disaster.
So let me take into my eyes the wasteful systems
and the cities where we live and die like plants in glass.
Let me take in the insane
and I'll light my insanity for the children.

In another scattered city on the coast
a mother sits at the edge of the land in the early evenings
to watch her children floating in a growing sea.

Each morning she goes inland to work
and hears talk of how the human world's insanity
is mounting, and the wings of the birds
are turning to sand.

She goes back to land's edge in the evenings
and watches the seagulls still fly
and the late violet sunlight detonate the clouds.
In a little cove where she built a table
of wood and bone,
she sets for her children a meal of flesh,
greens and fruits,
and she calls the children back to land's edge
to be renewed.

Under a sky full of questions, she tells them:
  Live for your bodies
  not for your fantasies:
  the only immortality
  is reproduction in life:
  though everything seems vain and vanishing
  dreams in blood are transmitted
  and flower.

And Narcissus says:
  Of beauty, only the monstrous kind
  can rearrange me. And dreams more often wilt
  or break, or get tangled in others and fade.
  And we're not so much flowers
  as links in a chain of errors born at the start of language
  that we're doomed to reprise.

A Narcissus who glimpses his Echo
in the mirror of a toxic sky,
in the bright abyss of photographs his Echo
dressed in the colors of a mechanized day . . .

My poem's land is woven, leafed.
And its words in their wandering inhabit a larger world
whose chemical sunsets look back at me when my eyes close.
You're strange in your meaning, they tell me.
On the radio, on my way to work, the lyricist sings,
"I live life like the captain of a sinking ship"

but that was years ago. And I know I used to sing
to weigh the vastness spilled by a hummingbird's flight
and not to explain any thing's intention.
I learned this language and am strange in it.
I speak in its verbs and nouns to see outside,
to hear others and take breaks from the rich silence
of being alone, the moment-to-moment
folding of wakefulness.

And the words in their wandering inhabit a larger world
and in me they have their exile.

Another stranger.
Whenever I looked for myself
in my meditations,
I found other people's faces, and when I looked
for them I found my younger self
meeting theirs for the first time.
Am I this point that travels?
This fragmentation?

Another stranger mangled
into being and propelled through years
into the passenger seat of a girl's car
traveling along a narrow, little-trafficked
country road, fields on either side of us extending
all the way to the horizon.

She had a small coffee for me
when she came to pick me up.
I hold the warm paper cup now
between cold fingers.
It's a clear cloudless day,
the sky massive.
I don't know where we're going.

She says a park, by a lake.
And in the passenger's side-mirror,
I see her dog in the back sticking her head
out the window, staring down the road with a calm
animal seriousness, the wind making indents
on her golden coat . . .

I am tired of my adjectives.
The world splits their shells and flows on.
I have to fall between my words
to reach the mirrors that repeat me.
In these spaces, my acts are my acts
even if I don't belong to me
and there's nothing left to clean the cuts in my voice.
Its blood-drips too are a language,
its bent branches,
even if I don't belong to me,

even if I'm the one to whom the pages
of the books that gave me their vocabulary

to get me here
have said:

> Write and you'll be.
> Read and you'll find.

> And to speak, you must act. Word
> and action are opposites that unite
> in meaning.

So I trade the lamp of my past
for each night lit by live and dead stars.
So when we are again Earth's victims,
and not its tomb-builders, let the past be new
and the future come like a storm giving back
what we decayed into its wind.

In the solitude that holds us,
there with the dead where all pronouns dissolve,
the stones continue their slow talk with the water.
And no one alive says to the dead: become me.
Yet the dead do.

On my days off
I read through pages of a song Darwish wrote
in a hospital in Texas:
He arrives where time is zero.
Death's representatives gather at his body's portals

and wait for his heart to stop.
He is not alive or dead in that whiteness
where void and being merge and lose their letters.
One day his mind disbands,
his "I" steps into the open
and doesn't return.

I sit years later immersed
in this spell he left on pages in a sick room
on days when he thought no new skies
again would greet him.
(Just between us ghosts,
you singer for those the victor's army
left on the field, harvester of your own cage and garden,
how good to think that you're older than the Earth now
and younger than this living me who writes
these letters down.)

Expand your attention, she would say.
It's your only limit.
On a rumpled mattress by a window with a view
of a street covered in snow
she said,
I love lying down in your gaze.
And I told her each of her movements
was a small addiction I had,
that I loved keeping her secrets.
And she said, Your sanity is my science.

What you want of me is yours
for however many nights or days we last . . .
Now sleep. Sleep
is a balm in winter.
Be calm and worthy of what you dream.

And I saw us at a party at the end of winter,
kissing in the hallway as everyone danced.
My hand slipped under your shirt, surprised
to be surprised again by your softness as your skin etched
its breath on my palm. We woke in different cities
and I wasn't dreaming I was dreaming. Outside,
the wind reminded me of my skin, and I reached
for your face in some strange field where the grass opened
and the sky played its rain.

And I saw the last evening on Earth.
On the last evening on Earth
we sever our days from the buildings and roads
and we sever our days from the water.
We don't count the maps laid behind us
or the ones left ahead, undrawn.
On the last evening we say goodbye to nothing
and find no time to end who we are.
Everything advances:
the place releases our wants
and exchanges its flora.

And I saw my father climb onto a bus
that took him north.
And as my mother and I walked out of the station
into a blurred crowd, he became a strange
distant world, though I didn't think of it
as we continued past street vendors
and beggars. (And as he stared out
through the window of the bus
at the desert he was entering
what did I become?)
As my mother and I crossed a pedestrian bridge
the cars below became water, the sky cleared
and I was alone again inside my days.

And I saw Nietzsche and Ali Ahmad Saïd
walking the bank of a polluted river,
not looking for hierarchies or poetry.
Their conversation a swarm of leaves
blowing over the factories.
Wrapped in winter coats
and far from the tenure of their tasks,
they followed the stream out of the city
and up, towards the ice.

And I saw Celan sedimenting his butchers
into his poem, saying:
You stripped off the flesh of my language.
Now I'm too awake to see what you see.

Vision is a light that crosses voids
or leads to madness.

And I saw myself many years later,
in another town, recovering from my mind's
unhinging. My thoughts having detached from me
were plunging unrestrained, toward nothingness.
A friend told me it would pass. That night I sat
in my pajamas on the fire escape's metal balcony,
drinking, smoking cigarettes at the clouds,
and listening to the clangs of the nearby train yard
as I waited for sleep. And when sleep
finally came, I woke up on an island
where the last of the flightless birds
watched a boat approaching . . .

But the mind is only smoke.
Let it drift into new selves a thousand ways.

Years after we met,
I keep remembering those birds of prey we saw
on our first walk in the woods, wounded
in their cages, the keepers feeding them mice in the tree-
filtered light.   Did their tendons dream of flying?
I'm so far from the start of my own dreamed alphabet
that my language has become a riddle to me.
One thread of sun is enough to pierce my day's shelter.
One thread of sun that changes flags and distant shores

where soldiers have built for me this era of forgetfulness.
Is there a country larger than its audience?
One smaller than its trash?
Our machines widen our habits
and the letters of a poem illuminate the guns we hung
on the gates of the seasons.

In a Mexico City café, we sit at a table and read.
Through my headphones flows a symphony
a dead man made from an algorithm,
and again in this Babylon whose veins
multiply at night, I'm at a loss to say what string
could pull me back to my first emptiness.
There aren't enough hours.
Our days are twisted,
scattered between news clips
and taxis. In the machine parts
I found no private morning
for my childish love to say its words.

But she sat next to me and held my palm up
like a child examining a glowing leaf
and said: The world is so much noise.
Your name calling mine is a winged needle
flitting above the markets and motorcades.
And your love is not childish.
We both know neither time
nor the space we travel through is ours.

This strange room we rented with strange coins
will be a temporary stage.
And don't worry if you're tired
of me wanting to be yours.
We don't belong to ourselves.
Only our senses possess in passing,
can hold us awhile in their thoughtless play.
Are you tired of me wanting
to be yours?

And I said, It's just that I keep trying to record
the early sunlight on my arm. Forgive me
if I'm quiet sometimes, if I don't
have words to tell you how the joy you take
from the sight of street dogs lounging in the heat,
by the avocado stands, eases my sleep
and haunts its dreams with visions
of you by a lake, at night,
watching in the distance the cyclopic buildings
people keep launching at the clouds.

We've grown older.
More doubtful of the weight and lightness at stake.
Now we can get on the road to Moscow or Damascus
and feel history's brushing gaze recording
and forgetting us.

Two stone doves land on a power line,
linger some seconds then flutter
into what's left of our lives.

Our days fold, fractured,
elliptical. My father once asked if I still
dreamt. You need to have dreams,
he said. Children could be your dreams.
You can watch them surprise you
the rest of your days.

But in the future
I see only a version of myself adrift
in replica cities
where too many dreams
already suffocate the air.
Leftover plastics blend with our skins
in this time between ashes and flowers.
Funhouses for hollow children bloom
where the old rain makers danced.
Here is where brilliant minds must grow.
Here where I learned to wear disguises
and lost track of my first selves.

Lost,
though some habits stayed.
For one I wasn't born
to know that I would fail.

I was born to love the storm cloud's shadow
and the collision of lives inside it.

We used to tell each other stories to go to sleep.
Lately I've relied on self-squandering:
You are not yours, I tell myself,
and it's useless to cling to a friend's or a lover's voice.
No moon or piece of ground
is yours for long. So leave your shadow
and the shadow of your words in the rooms
you walk through, leave them on the balconies
of apartments at 2 AM, with a party still going inside,
filling the walls with laughter and talk of how we'll fare
in the coming rearrangement of the sand.

I've lost my first self
and my others have blurred in my wandering.
And what has lust done to us, love?
In its bliss it always promised more
and marched us blindly, anxious, looking
for the next strange window to wake up next to.

The city is a nerve cell of crossed wants and we're splinters from the
poem of survival and the poem of dust. And we would've been stagnant
had the sound of engines and the ocean's crash not made us see we were
inventions. Had as children we not sensed in the pages of old books some
kind of eternity, had our senses longed less for others, we would've been
ordinary

had pleasure been enough to seal our sleep.

So I return to this land of accidents
in whose cemeteries trash-delighted winds
brush the grass: land of my poem woven
with our scattered aims
and perfect in its aimlessness.

And of this land I have the magic
between stimuli and vision.
And I have the eucalyptus
contemplating the shade of its image.
I have prophets' and bookkeepers' voices
that blend into my day's mutations.
I have the chimera the world appeared as in a dream
to a man who slept on the mouth of a cave
and I have the red hand prints he left on a stone.
I have the stone-piles of meanings
that lie under words
made by clay tongues that held on
to what they could of the weather:
called it diamond dust, ball lightning, acid rain.

And if this poem's land is not enough
I have its echo in my ear as I walk
in the mornings to work.
Months have gone by since we moved
to the house in the desert.

We part ways and meet again in the evenings.
On weekends I go to the park
by the court house
and sit under a tall cottonwood
in whose top branches
two owls have made a home.

Alone there, my last hour and I
wave to each other across the emptiness
I've yet to fill.
And we converse in silence
in the dry summer of this western town we've landed in
where I speak of myself to no one for days
and see my reflection in only the trees that shade
the churches and tourist shops.
My last hour tells me to shadow absence
and to not rush into a struggle
my heart didn't first dream.
It tells me to follow it
to a village it has yet to build.
That it waits patiently there
with the last of my images . . .

But not today. For today is Sunday
and the weather is clear,
and the asphalt simmers with noon.
It's Sunday, and the night is warm.
The girls' dresses decorate the plaza

and no one but me
waits for me in my hour.

But who exactly is it that waits?

My self is a bounded mess.
A rabble of wants that avail themselves of a mind
moving in two tongues.
To it, I say: With words I shaped you
in this animal body
and with words
you hold steady while the day
weaves through you, rearranging.
And you made me
and made what I'll become.

So paint me with your astonishment
and your ignorance.
Show me in your afternoons
walking by trash fields in the city of childhood,
standing in decrepit buses full of peddlers and workers
as you rode every week to the art school.
Be faithful to the grid your species grafted
to the soil. On the asphalt our drives are free.
They can roam through any glass display
and build for their lust and anxiety a city of dolls.

Who else could sing here
but you, Dionysus?
You who laughs at Narcissus and invites him to dance.
You whose stomach this world can't turn.
. . . So sing!
Maybe the journalists will find the elephant's
residency papers under a Humvee's tire.
Maybe the whales we are sending to No One
will engrave their music in membrane-glows the earth
has yet to invent.
Maybe the plastic in the oceans will melt and complete its destiny
and maybe the mosquitoes in summer
will make peace with my nights.

Sing and say:

I am the smoke-filled air and the lung.
I'm a symphony of melodies that dart
and bait each other like last thoughts before sleep.
I am the temple and the vandal.

While Darwish's pages whisper:
I own nothing for anything to own me.
He whispers to us dwellers of this day that swarms
in its own time,
a womanly day,
flexible,
oceanic in gesture . . .

And more days like this one will come.
Days whose air and birds
will ignore the names we gave them
in our efforts to housetrain the sky.
No one will feel like committing suicide or leaving:
There will be time for that later, time enough
to even grow old and die.

I own nothing for anything to own me.
It's as if conditions for the existence
of breathing, thinking beings
were too narrow for aimless, love-obsessed lyricists:
minds molded by visions that found them young
and kept them so.
Hopelessly hopeful, they see a beautiful thing
and immediately try
to coach silence a song.

I own nothing for anything to hold me to its center.
I have a flood to swim and drown in
and a date in the sand with one of my defeats.
And the stories we survived?
How do we proceed in the cities they erected?
Redecorate the windows? Spend our time
crisscrossing moons and empty stations?
How do we walk above the history of plot?
Begin from zero? Break alliances?
"No dead ever came back to tell us the truth."

So again I ask myself: who are you?

Are you the boy born from soil that was fertilized
by killers and victims
long before your father's people settled in their villages
to enter the end of their era
with calmness and candles?

Or maybe a mixture
of this language the Empire gave you
and the gift of displacement your parents launched you into
with the best intentions?

Maybe a drifter who left
not bound for war
but to see the flood up close
and lost his way home?

It makes sense that books
left in you their musk and phantoms
as if you'd glimpsed in the depths of the story
the voice of the conquered who know how to talk in lamplight
after dinner, for every gathering is precious
and shouldn't be wasted on irony or posturing.
There's no time for that when the present is dismantling
your place and language.

It makes sense that you were changed
when you learned as a child about the telephone.
I remember you pretending to speak on it
while your mother watched and laughed
and you laughed with her,
the receiver bigger than your head.
Strange, intoxicating, this idea
that a stranger might be out there and would listen
to your thoughts about the houses and street dogs
and the colors of the ants
through this machine.
And as your words gathered in you their twisted lifetimes
what did you become?

I remember us smoking with a friend
in a vacant baseball field.
Another mild December day in California.
Your 28th birthday, the blue sky promising a whole
life's worth of losses.
Life is a flow I intensify and define,
you heard Death say.
And we sat on a shaded patch of grass
against the outfield fence, drank our beers
and peeled the oranges we'd brought.

When 30 came around
you almost didn't notice the morning fog
swallowing a hummingbird's song in the yard.

You were at your mother's house for the holidays
after a long year in the desert where you and your lover
mangled each other's love to absurdity.
Already you were saying goodbye to the streets
where you walked to the movies after work
and dreamt of future seasons
and you almost didn't notice the green
of the hummingbird's wings
splashing the day's allegro with vanishing.

But a voice reminded you:
Don't rush to see tomorrow.
Live your tomorrow now, and remember
to notice the way your body merges
with new bruises. Enter this hour slowly
knowing it guarantees neither exit
nor safe passage. Take time to leave
the city for a season, and take time
to take off your shoes and socks
so you can walk barefoot on the grass.

This is your summer.
Tend to it as it befits a poet skilled at labyrinths
for the joyful and despondent to get lost in.
A poet who reveres the coolness of the bell
yet is undermined by his need for sweetness,
even one moment of tenderness in night's impersonal pockets,
one warm touch to illuminate the plaza

and render the noise of the crowd mere background
for the spectacle of possible things.

Your summer happens on a common day
chosen for no reason than the clouds being high up
and scattered, softening the sun here and there.

Tend to it well.
Don't just wander from shelter to shelter.
The summer air is made for those in love with lingering,
those who know health is not a goal but a means.
And use your words with care now that you know
"they are as valuable as rope
with nothing to be tied to."

Your summer appears in a time of disaster and hesitation
in a world of splintered seasons where the old ways
are shedding layers constantly,
putting on the skins of systems
and new colonies of being.

We read about the dying of the oceans in our living rooms.
Warmed ourselves with wine and strings of light we hung
on the windows. Kept our circle in the night and talked about life's
webs of love and disappointments, shared videos of old scientists
who spoke to us from toxic trash dumps in the past. Kept our circle
and imagined the species that would burst from us, talked about it
late into the hours that belonged to the rats in the alley.

In the morning, we said goodbye after tea
and left each other to our separate habits.
And I returned to my poem's land, changed in my absence.

The last time I was here, I was asking time to stay
and let me remember where my life had been.
Asked that it stand still enough for my ears
to recall the laughter of my closest friends,
those loyal companions scattered in different towns now.
I asked that it wait for me to record
the scent of a loved one's hair as we embrace
outside the station, saying:

Time, it would cost you nothing.
It'd be like forgetting a barren moon orbiting a dead planet
or a cigarette you tossed on a drive through Texas
on your way to meet a long and dancing California
that you had never seen.

Time, let me breathe deep and forget you.
So that my day becomes a season in the northern forest
and when it's over it'll be as if I'd woken from a beautiful dream.
I'll catch up with you again the next morning
over coffee
and we'll speak as friendly elements a while.

All I want is a continual re-making of the world.

So I sift through my personas to see
which one to wear today.

Maybe I could be the naturalist in me.
And I'll pause on my early walk
to memorize the air-ballet of flies
above a dead coyote on the road
or stoop to contemplate the frogs that sprout
from leaves after rain, recording in my notebook
their skin's carbuncular patterns.
Or I'll spot a tortoise as it crosses
the dirt path flanked by trees
that leads to my cabin.
The creature senses me from yards away
and freezes.
I keep my movements soft,
un-sudden, so it won't startle and retreat into its shell.
And it doesn't retreat completely,
maybe sensing no aggression on my part
as it watches me, stone-still,
and my fingertips brush its carapace,
feel the compact, reptilian body breathing inside.
And I'd spend many days in many woods and meadows
studying the self-contained animals maneuvering around our roads.
And I'd find shelter beneath trees and overpasses,
and hunch over my pages many hours there
archiving the shapes life takes on. And when I return
to the company of fellow humans in some town

I'll look with fresh eyes at the trees and concrete surrounding me there,
exchange some passing talk with a man reading his shadow in the park
and see how words enable us to share a mind.
And I'll watch the cars and traffic signs and wonder:
Why does man assume a loftiness over things wild
as if he himself were not a wild thing, his laws and borders
mere straps in a straitjacket that tears with his mutations?

Or maybe I could be the hedonist in me
and I'll let my friend kiss my thighs
and let language rest in peace on the floor
as I forget myself in my welcoming body
and a strong summer air bathes the sheets
and the bed holds us like an altar
far from the underworld and far
from everything dull.
Later, on the patio, we eat the Earth's magic plants
as daylight turns languorous and golden.
A stranger who has come for us tonight
conjures from a cello a sonata
as the first guests walk through the door
with their potions and their perfect bodies . . .

Or maybe I could be the teacher in me,
and say to one who comes to me with questions:
    Learn well to stray from my advice.
    The further you can stray from my advice and thrive,
    the freer, more virtuosic you'll become.

Or even better, I could be the father in me,
and write to a child who will carry my life for me
a letter I'll entrust to the flux of the seasons.

My father, I'll write, knew as little as I did
when he set out to harvest his spring.
The joys and difficulties of each day
were written already in his childhood
and the way his youth gave itself to a woman
who woke in him an urge to fall.
It took distances, the slow work
of building a home in a strange country.
This is the legacy in your limbs and language.
Take of it what you think will last
and go to the fields, hungry for us as they are.
Look for shadows
and shine light in them at least once a day,
see how far the hallways they conceal extend:
they might lead to open meadows or useful ladders
or gardens housing monsters you might have to meet.
Keep an eye out for water sounds and birds.
Beauty will carry your desire for you.
Your words can take you where you want
and your body is your carriage and your clock.
Be tender every chance you can.
Eat a bit of your death every day
and help others eat from theirs if you have time.

And when time comes, bury me well and deep
and leave me to the flux of the seasons.

Or maybe I could be the adventurer in me,
readied and ready for my death.
Ready day and night and every hour
as I test the world's edges in search of my limits.

And like a good adventurer
I won't fear asking for directions
and won't fear discarding them
if I hear a song from deep in some field.
I'll be prepared for any encounter,
unwavering in my attention,
my curiosity a brave bird.
I'll improvise across borders
and in the cities go in search of night's gates.
And when I am alone again in whatever
temporary shelter I've found or made,
I'll pull my self out of myself
and weigh the various gears of it,
stand to test for stability,
see that it's light enough,
dancer enough,
before wandering on . . .

Or I could be the Death-obsessed poet.
And I'll say to my Death:

Why do you stare at me
from the clearing outside my door?
You stare and stir the mutations inside me.
I see you watching from the glossy tops of the leaves,
waving from the sheer curtains of the kitchen window.
I have many interiors still to place in my exterior.
After I'm rid of them, I'll meet you gladly,
maybe by some grassy cliff-side
or by the window of a rented room
somewhere between Hell and Zipolite
on Earth's wedding day.

Or sit with me awhile to watch the crowds
as they pass by this small café.
And say: how did the old masters face you
when you took them in?
Was it a smooth fluid merging
the way sugar cubes dissolve in steaming tea?
Or did you have to swat aside their brave
and futile clinging to the mortal world?

But Death's only answer
will be the silence in the sand.

And I, mad with a mind that won't relent,
will insist and say,
I first saw you in a vacant house.
You were sitting on the edge of every object in the room,
your breath floating through the clutter,
rousing the dust of those who had lived there.
And you followed me out into the garden
where I sensed your alchemy
tying me to the air, allowing the sun to seep
into the bones of living things, giving the shrieks
of the youngest petals volume.

You who release the ground and the sky for us,
since we can open your doors from anywhere at all,
tell me: is there one that leads back
to that first grain of sand that helped me dream?

But Death's only answer will be
the flap of a bird rising from the asphalt
into a sweltering sky.

And I, mad with an urge to linger in my briefness,
will insist and say: Death, if the dust sings
does it merely go back to being dust?

Does not our language carry our minds beyond us
even as you clarify the land on a normal day?
And there are dead

who shine with more life
than those living who drag their own bodies.

But Death's only reply will be
the gaping mouth of a dragon fruit flower
nectar-filled beneath a desert moon.

Outside my window
a morning filled with possible days
yields two young pear trees swaying in early sunlight.
Yields the sound of a helicopter above the town
and the noise of the market
at the bottom of the hill.

Tired of my questioning,
I will let my steps take me to the shadow
of some buildings on a busy plaza
and to an idea about the ephemerality
between coincidence and beauty.

I'll walk on the main promenade,
in the stream of foreigners and vendors,
side alleys teeming with shouts and jingles in the afternoon.
The day goes by in a kaleidoscope of faces
and my steps take me to an old cantina
where a friend sits with two beers
and a pack of cigarettes, and asks,

Are you prepared, my friend,
to be at peace with the unknown?

And I answer, I am a plant that was fed to the wind
after my land was sold for its secrets:
I am to make of the unknown a home.

And we'll drink to the wakefulness of bodies at night
and go to a courtyard where a band is playing
festive songs of longing and heartbreak
and the dance floor teems.
We'll take the hands of two girls sitting
at a table by a stone column
and merge with the frenzy of bodies
moving in the sea of notes that wears the air,
our limbs interlacing and parting, skirts
and locks of hair rising and falling like waves in a storm.

My cells are awake with longing.
My partner's waist feels supple and strong against my palm
and as she spins everything suddenly feels possible.
It seems life glows eternally and knows.

"Don't forget your appointment," a voice whispers.

But I, mad with an itch to unearth what I'm becoming,
remember to forget the void that hosted the moon's conception

so I can dedicate my hour to praising
with my whole doomed body
the trumpet's sweet sadness unlacing the evening.

And I remember the sea gate
where I have a date with one of the defeats,
at the edge where my words will leave me
to tell their own stories.

Death, you are the wax
that seals what never got written.
I am left to guess at the names.

We dance through our days
in the swimming light
towards you.

Weaving through traffic,
our voices yearn for each other
and in memory our deeds escape
your clumsy victory:
fingers reaching through strange
painful rings,
tips that melt away.

I take the clock's gears
empty of time

and make a necklace of them
that will reflect the sun's reflection
on the water.

Many deaths poured into my being here.
And the blood of my dead is alive in my limbs.
My dead dance in me tonight, across from you,
in the swimming light.

With so much coursing through me,
from endlessness to endlessness,
who am I to lament my transformations
or deny you your clumsy victory?

But Death's only answer
will be the memory of an ocean with no wind
as I exit the courtyard
into the cool, adulterated air.

Or I could be no one today.
And the outside will resemble me a lot
even as I resemble nothing.
My history will become a forgotten breeze
diffused into the worldspace we breathe,
my "I" a centerless network of perceptions.

But this freedom won't survive the day.
Soon enough, the world will mold me into shape

as I start wandering and others see in me
what they want to see of themselves.
And I will say to them:

> I am a mirror of myself
> made by my history's failure to sustain me,
> so I let the threads that tied my senses to my memory
> burn in the labyrinth of days.

But they won't understand me.
My homeland is a language with no meaning.
Beauty swims under its letters and breaks through them
like a whale bursting the face of the sea.
I follow this language out into the open air
and when the terrible sublimity of straying
tires me,
I return to whatever identity
will hide my nothingness from strangers
who demand a tribe and origin
they can look for on a list,
and I become what I want of my history's fragments
in the distances of singing
and I tell them:

> I come from a mutilated country
> where lush mountains hide their insects' innocence
> from the light
> and blood fertilizes the mango trees.

I had a field of sugarcane there
before centuries of human invention
tore through its soil.
It was next to a turquoise river
where the old gods floated by each morning,
naked and laughing like children.

And after these others tire of listening to me and leave,
I return to the magic of walking alone without agendas
in the narrow cobbled streets of a small town
while the people are sleeping
and no one is waiting for me when my language
seeks a name to hold to.

My steps, which sound too lonely in the sleepers' ears,
are fine companions in the clear silence
where I stroll
and let the story that once danced around me
stay where I left it, an ash heap on some sandy beach,
not caring if it's there when I come back to re-enter my biography.
I'll sit on a bench on some corner to wait
for a bus that will take me to another nowhere.

For now, I walk lightly, without a hurry
like the unemployed do.
It's early noon
and I stop to watch my shadow watching me
over my shoulder.

Then I hear the voice of a woman behind me ask:
Were you waiting for me?

I turn and tell her:
I was waiting for another "I"
to tell me what I've become.
I wondered if this other
would be a bird in someone's yard
or one of those eucalypti
trembling with breezes.

And she mumbles:
Another man lost in his days . . .

And before I can finish telling her
that I'm not lost but only watching my shadow watching me
as I wait for my cells to grow hungry for expiring again,
she has already turned around and started walking back
to a rooftop garden in the city she came from.
And because I am loyal to life whenever possible
we make a truce over tomorrow's uncertainty
and go together in search of a late-night diner.

We shared a handful of breaths here, once,
on this very corner,
just as a wind
was sweeping the letters of a poem

toward the snowfields
north of the future.

———

When you left
I went back to a rooftop restaurant
in the other country
and watched my solitude color the air above the tables.
Without you my name changed, and my hands
forgot the scent of morning alibis against time and its army.
I asked my day to hold still and let me collect the fingers
of my writing hand
as I exchange some passing talk
with the wind that's carrying to other places the plans we made.

Now every morning I wake to my body's disjunctions again,
make coffee and skim over the news,
then patiently write to the meter of absent buffalo herds
a line in the poem of grass.

I've become one of these makeshift men again.
A stranger at the airport
on my way to pay a visit to my ruins
(still under construction).

But my body is still the elements' metaphor for dreaming.
So I beg my imagination:

　　Persist. You are my liveliness.
　　Refresh yourself in the fountains our wars built
　　and in the invention of a day inside a night.
　　Stiffen your back and launch your threads again
　　like a flag abandoned in language's land.

　　Your words will open other doors.
　　Don't rush through the clearings allotted us.
　　We both know we can't bargain with the Lord of Days.

　　Land from your lonely definitions of the world
　　and learn from the communion of plants.
　　Land and be free.

It's a short drive to the sierra
from this small city I found in the south.
Before you know it, the clouds are a few feet away,
floating in the ravine next to the road as we pass.

I stop and walk down a slope until soon
I reach an open ledge where I stand and listen to the pines
for a while. They cover the mountain
and move in unison with the wind,
the whole earth in them breathing
and I one of its roving particles, watching.

From this rock overlooking the valley,
death seems justified, that constant
companion on the other side of time.
How else would all this beauty exist?
How good that we die.

After the hike, we return to the cabin
and warm our thoughts by the stove,
flames lit under a pot of water.
And it's good to think I have today what tomorrow will make
of these fragments of mine.

And though I don't belong to me
I don't need eternity to be alive.

I need only to speak
and to sing in this day
where I get up from the page and put on clothes.

All I want is the continual re-making of the world.
The wind that rends the heat apart.

The ripened fruit

falling

Acknowledgments

Sections of this book appeared previously in the *Boston Review*, *Sparkle & Blink*, the *Porter House Review*, the *Charles River Journal*, and the Academy of American Poets' Poem-A-Day Series.

The Author would like to give special thanks to Eric Hayes and Katherine Johnson of the Tasajillo Writers' Residency, The MacDowell Colony, and the University of Iowa's MFA in Creative Writing program, for their support during different stages of the writing of this book.

OTHER TITLES FROM THE SONG CAVE: